DIÁLOGOS
BOOKS

The Light
That Shines
Inside Us

Marguerite Guzmán Bouvard

DIÁLOGOS
BOOKS
New Orleans

The Light That Shines Inside Us

Copyright © 2013 by Marguerite Guzmán Bouvard

ISBN: 978-1-935084-38-9

Book design by Bill Lavender.

Cover photo and design by Jacques Bouvard.

DIÁLOGOS
BOOKS
New Orleans

Acknowledgements

With gratitude to the magazines in which these poems first appeared:

Noah Charles Pierce, SPC in *Magnolia, a Journal of Socially Engaged Literature, Vol. 2, 2012.*

Bougainvillea in *The Poetic Bond, Willowdown Books, U.K.*

Hymns in *Tiferet*

Silence, The Art of Living, The First Weapons of War, Ludmilla, Meeting Egypt, The Book of Wisdom, in *Istanbul Literary Review.*

Still in Combat, Night, Of Time and Breath, in *The Drunken Boat.*

The Rilke Walk and Journey, *in Prose Poem Project.*

Val Rosandra in *Gemeni Magazine.*

Ahmed Kathedra, Somalia, Resurrection, Poem for Guy Muffat, My French Uncle, Woman with Seascape, A Silver Bracelet, in *Journal of Kentucky Studies.*

The Island Beyond Our Laws, in *Raving Dove.*

The Last Room, Human Landscape, The Church of St German-des-Pres, The World, Trieste, in *Louisiana Literature.*

Hopi Ceremonial Sash in *City Lights; an Anthology of Poetry and Art, Beachcomber Press.*

Addressing the Mountain, in *Journal of Humanities, Art and Aging.*

Summer and The Plains Dreaming in *Third Wednesday Press.*

Children in *Future Eyes, Pale House.*

Storia in the *Deronda Review*

The Sundarbans Tiger Preserve in *Redwood Coast Review.*

We Are One

Human Landscape

REVERENCE

THE TREES HOMILY

The Light That Shines Inside Us

The universe is smaller than a butterfly's wing in the boundless expanse of the heart.

Mahmoud Darwish

We Are One

Silence

You gave us many gifts:
the silence of early morning
with the cuckoo's two notes,
raucous crows, the drone
of occasional planes reminding us
of distance, when we can hear
our own voice, for everyone
has a voice inside them.
You gave us the silence
of deep nights when we can listen
to the breathing of our loved one
and to the women in the Congo
who are afraid to tell their stories
of how they were invaded
by the faceless again and again,
while the men who tried to protect
them were shot, to the children
in Afghanistan who were sold,
our abandoned veterans who sleep
in doorways. Remember that you
are in time's corridors, a journey
where you will reach understanding.
Do not run away from yourself.
You will see strife and mercy
all around. There will always be
wars, the barricades of those
who pile up treasure, the arrogant
who want to be celebrated. But
there are no real boundaries.
We are all one.
We are not alone.

Specialist Noah Charles Pierce

When he returned from the war
they called him a killer.
He was not a murderer.
He befriended a child, gathered

the limbs of his fellow soldier
who was blown up beside him,
lost some of his hearing from the blast,
obeyed his colonel's orders to gun down

a man driving into the Green Zone
who turned out to be a physician.
When he came home, the weight
of his guilt, displacement and pain

was invisible. He didn't come home.
He was still in Iraq. The people
in his town couldn't hear the nightmares
that haunted him or his heart

pounding at sudden noises.
They couldn't understand how he left his house
to protect his parents and his sister
from his anger, closed the door of his apartment

to release his sorrow. Then one night
he drove to the mine dumps
near his favorite fishing spot,
wrote "Freedom isn't Free"

on the dashboard of his truck
beside the nine medals of honor
closing yet another door
to liberate his own life.

The First Weapons of War

A poet asks me to translate the word
ethnocentrisim into French.
At first I am puzzled, then I recall
conversations in Paris and how I remained
silent, knowing it was useless to engage people
whose credo is s*ang ou sol*, blood
or country of origin. I used to tell my students
"Read *Mein Kampf* not for content,
but just to circle words that throb
in the gut." *Pure Blood* they circled,
primitive, sponger, only an ape.
So it is for people today who are born
in France and speak French, but can never truly
be French because their parents
came from North Africa.
So it is that cities fracture
into territories: the ones where young men
idle on streets that lead nowhere
and sometimes burn cars, the chic
arroundissments where slogans flare
like marauding winds, *Unruly immigrants
are a menace to the French culture.*
Does blood really have different colors
when it flows from a wound?
Always the power, the hidden
violence of words.

Ludmilla

I have placed my cancer
in a drawer and do not want
to think about it

She just returned from rehab.
The few nurses didn't have time
for her. Now she is back
in her apartment, her husband
dead, her son in another state
who doesn't care. She lives among
strangers, her reality is beyond
them, her memories of dawns
she savored and a darkness
that enfolded her;
denounced during the war
and sent to a concentration camp
when she was a teenager, her job
sorting dead bodies. After the war
she married wealth and then chose
poverty and love, settled
in different countries where
she was the language of their home.
I will end my life in my little world
with my paintings, books, photos.
The places we pass by
that may seem small
are where courage and grace
bloom like perennials
with their own light.

Trieste

Is a place where sea and sky are one,
where languages mingle
with the gestures of its peoples;
Austrian, Italian, Slovene, Croat,
where the Carso's wind-swept
stones are the pages of an ancient book,
is the place where my mother swam
by the Palace of Miramar, splashing the guards.
Trieste is the place where my grandfather
played the violin before leaving for the trenches
and an early appointment with death,
where Sunday afternoons my great-grandfather's
villa on the Via Palladio, throbbed
with the bustle of generations.
Trieste is the place where the Piazza Unitá borders
the generous arms of the harbor
and where so many years ago,
I cradled my new cousin Mirjana whose father
was washed up from yet another battlefield.
Trieste is where the wind changes
its moods, and war and love write their messages
on the multiples of our being; the Balkan's
fury still lapping at its shores, and the somnolent
afternoons when we gather with our children
and grandchildren beneath the apricot trees
in my cousin Maria-Teresa's garden.
Trieste is the history I carry
in my bones, a geography of light.

Still in Combat

There are scenes   that never leave
the mind   gathering up   the limbs
of a comrade   opening   a car door
only to see   a dead woman
with her children   the merciless heat
of a desert   reappearing
on a beach. There are   sounds
remaining   no one else   can hear
sparked   by a door   slamming,
the whine   of a vacuum cleaner.
There are fears   of open spaces   a picnic
in the middle   of a meadow
unease   at people   walking too
close behind   at being
in a crowd   night   after night
going to sleep   and waking up
with the ghosts   of the killed
feeling   like a failure
for having been   unable   to protect
fallen comrades   there is   no membrane
between life   and death
after returning   from a war.

The Castle at Miramare

The broad central esplanade leading towards the sea wall
is where prince Maximillian, brother of Emperor Franz Josef
once walked with his beloved wife, Carlotta. His passion was
gathering a variety of trees, but Napoleon goaded him into
conquering Mexico. He died at Chapultepec, entering the
kingdom of history where tyranny and tender shoots mingle.
Grounds where few venture, are the province of time and
serenity where trees from every corner of the world create
yet another world and conflicts disperse into the green air.

The Rilke Walk

A narrow path etches the cliffs above the Adriatic at Duino, celebrating a beloved poet sheltered by a prince in his castle, where Rilke wrote, *all that/soundless landscape under its clouded/ or clear destiny –all this came before you.** Despite the tapestry of green rising on one side, the foliage brushing the gravel path, gatherings of limestone rocks dominate the cliffs. Everywhere they greet us, communities of holy men, with concave cheeks, deep in reflection, carrying the burdens of invading armies, of kings anointed and deposed, soldiers whose bones have disappeared, the tears of the mothers. High above fishing nets, untouched by the ceaseless parade of nations, with their striations carved by steady drops of rain, they are a presence of so many thousands of years, a silence calling us above the sea's changing lights, the swish of boats, the flicker of our brief passage.

*Duino Elegies: The Third Elegy, Rainer Maria Rilke,.

Night

Reflections sculpt the room
from the long window:
a half open door,

light from a single lamp.
The mountain bares
its silvery sheen and immensity

enters, the jet-blue
velvet of space
against the window.

The blanket is flung back
where the sweet warmth
of skin thrills the palm,

where news from the day's
trenches casts shadows
and silently, grief slips in.

Of Time and Breath

For Elizabeth

We lingered on a green mountain slope --
just you and I in the bronzed
light, the air stilled,
time holding its breath,

although I knew you were in a hospital room
your sigh floating
like a feather above
the swish of footsteps.

But now we two were wayfarers
sharing our stories,
as if we had slipped free
from the sheaths of our distant

cities. Your voice was as steady
as the brushstrokes on your canvases
while I placed my hand
on your shoulder and spoke

of the journey beyond this mountain
that neither of us could chart.
Then I woke up.
One week later you died.

Val Rosandra

Start with a highway rising above
the skyline of buildings, then take the bypass
that brings you past Grandi Motori,
drive through small villages
with their stone walls shading the road
and you will arrive at Bagnoli
where you walk into the canyon,
of Val Rosandra as if you were back
in the beginning. Butterflies
greet us, writing their calligraphy
in the air, on the river's low murmur.
Among the bushes and trees are ruins
of Roman aqueducts, stones whisper
stories of empire and water
that flowed to Trieste.
An ancient tree leans over a boulder
serrated by moss, a sign rises
on the slopes reminding us
that a border once crossed the top
of the canyon and opened
one day a year when Josef Broz Tito,
head of the Politburo
in Yugoslavia proclaimed the Day
of Friendship: Italians walking
into his country, Croats,
Serbs and Slovines entering Italy
to celebrate each others' families.
In the Val Rosandra we are part of
history, the earth
is our skin, the language --
pulsing of cicadas.
There are no other sounds.

Inscriptions of Light

Václav Hável, 1936–2012

Czechoslovakia, a country of spires, music
and learning was crushed
by a blizzard of gunfire, a stream
of tanks only to be revived decades later

by a playwright, Václav Hável, who refused
to bow before the conqueror.
Now, in once empty streets, memories
of a luminous chapter,

Hável's Velvet Revolution, awaken
crowds of people filling public squares,
local churches, in villages and small towns.
The Plaque on Národni Třida, that honors

the demonstrators of November 17th, 1989,
celebrates the times and passing
of the first president, Václav Hável,
the mingling of joyful

and tragic events. Votive candles
and thank you notes are placed
at the statue of Saint Wenceslas,
Hável's namesake. Václav Hável showed

the Czech people and the world,
that even in the most horrific circumstances,
anything is possible as he welcomed
the millions of Sudeten Germans,

that were expelled from Germany, healed
cultural and religious differences.
Before he died he wrote, *I'm convinced
that my existence*

*—has ruffled the surface of Being,
and that Being has a memory…
and thus my insignificance, a dissident,
a prisoner, a president,*

*a pensioner, a hermit and an alleged
hero, but secretly a bundle
of nerves, will remain
somewhere here.*

Throughout his life
he showed us that power
lies not in fame or in greatness,
but in a thousand small acts.

Ahmed Kathrada

I chat with two young South Africans
who discuss their favorite singers and their jobs,
but when I mention Ahmed Kathrada
who was close to Nelson Mandela
their faces turn blank. I'm in the wrong
generation. Who remembers this towering
figure, Ahmed Kathrada,
prisoner no. 468/64 locked in his cell
from 4:00 p.m. to 5:00 a. m.
Because he is Indian he was allowed
one pair of long pants and socks
while Nelson Mandela was in shorts
and remained barefoot in the biting cold
of Robben Island. There were eight
political prisoners besides them, four
illiterate, but Ahmed said, "one
to teach, one to learn." Who recalls
that more than a quarter of a century
they were at hard labor there with shovels
and pick axes, yet planning the road
to reconciliation. Meanwhile
there were massacres, Sharpeville,
with hundreds murdered, including children.
Ahmed and Mandela had no books
or newspapers but they were learning
wisdom and endurance. When they faced
President De Klerk, they bargained
for a new South Africa
and did not give in. They insisted on
a country that is inclusive,
the end of Apartheid. Mandela
became President, Ahmed Kathrada
served as Mandela's parliamentary counselor.
Sixteen years have flown by,

two million houses were built, but who
remembers this man with
his quiet dignity, educated in the school
of hunger and abuse, who has risen
above hatred and divisions,
cities where adult servants
were called "boy," or "girl,"
where shacks in Soweto
had neither water nor electricity
and where tourists now flock.

The Island Beyond Our Laws

Is where the light falls down
like a dead tree,
and night is a vulture
flapping its hungry wings,

where we strip off a name
with the person's clothes;
the ailing grandfather,
the man who held his son on his lap,
the one who drank tea
with his family in the afternoon,
who had brothers and sisters
that loved him, a mother who waited
for him at dusk,

where death is kept at bay
and language flayed
on the runaway horse
of euphemisms;
"enhanced interrogations"
"stress techniques"
"no touch"
"self imposed pain,"

is where my country's heart
pulses behind the barbed wire
of fear, its soul
disappeared like the laws
we abandoned with such ease.

The Diaspora

They flee from Syria to Jordan, Lebanon
and Turkey -- Syria where the days once
moved like symphonies
allegro

vivace;
clattering plates, a car door
slamming, footsteps rushing down
a sidewalk near streets clanging

with traffic. Then
the adagio sustenuto
of arrivals; a brimming counter,
a desk piled with unfinished tasks,

corridors with passing colleagues,
upturned faces in a schoolroom,
books ready to be opened.
The days had their maps

of neighborhoods, towns, cities,
each home with their own numbers for
the lento
of evenings surrounded

by family, the hours
in a mosque where people bowed
and lifted their hearts without seeing
the sudden strafing, the arc of their country

vanishing as they fled
into the blank pages of days,
unknown languages, improvising
life's discordant music.

Storia

A gravel path winds through
wild shrubs, dense thickets
of trees. There are no footsteps,
just the clamorous buzz
of cicadas, wave upon
wave. Rocks jut out among
openings of tall grasses, holding
eons among the leaves
temporary appearance.
The path leads to an empty
garrison devoid of thudding
boots, the rifle's crack.
Demarcations are cancelled
by oblivion, Slovenia blurs
into Italy, borders shift beneath
my skin. Butterflies
weave the air with their colors,
hold the beauty of the moment
in their wings.

Living History

In the West Bank, near Bethlehem
farmers grow their crops
on terraces, among tombs

and ruins of ancient
civilizations. Water flows
through a Roman irrigation system,

among the tranquility
of generations, while its neighbor
will build a network

of fences, walls, razor wire,
and patrol roads deep in that valley --
for its security, where both sides

have mutilated bodies as well as
Psalms, the look of holiness,
and one side wishes

to become the country
it remembers. I too have known
borders, where boundaries

were drawn by strife,
where my family's estate
that thrived for generations

was destroyed, defined
by a new language,
where love and hate

grow as easily as dandelions,
and the ones who remained,
became internal

refugees, aliens, in one
of many places where
our worlds collide.

The Vengeance of the Gods

In the Zócalo, Mexico City's giant square,
cracks open, buildings tilt and buckle
over Aztec ruins. The cathedral
constructed with their stones
is falling. Its dominion challenged
by the city that lies below it,
the Aztec, *Mexica,* capital,
Tenochtitlán, with its monolith
of the moon goddess Coyolxauhqui, the sacred
precincts of temples and palaces.
Calmécac, a school of *Mexica* nobles,
extends beneath the courtyard
of Mexico's education ministry.
Today the remains are laid bare:
Tenochtitlán's ball court for a ritual
ball game based on the *Mexica's*
religion, and the place where the last king,
Cuauhetamoc, was hung by the Spaniards,
his people ravaged by smallpox.
But they have not disappeared.
Their pyramids still hold the sky
outside the city, where *Mexicas*
pay homage on their steps.
In this world, conquerors are just
conquerors, hold not the millennia
of what they tried to destroy, but only
a small slice of time in their hands.

Syria

Outside a hospital in Aleppo
a little boy sits on a bench,
waiting to be admitted.
His blood stained neck and clothes,
the bandage on his head
do not obscure the mixture
of innocence and pain
in his uncertain smile.
The world around him
is no longer recognizable;
the roar of gunfire, the helicopters'
sudden clatter, concrete rubble
filling the streets he can no longer
walk, burned out houses.
Where is his mother who washed
his face, his grandmother
who cooked special treats, his father
that disappeared in plumes
of smoke? It's as if
he were on another planet,
without laughter or dreams,
just the bench where he waits
for hours without knowing more
than this unfathomable present.

Territory

We see them swoop among
trees, branches, meadows, against low clouds –
from a distance. But now between

the clapboards of an exterior wall,
rises a faint chorus of newborns.
A yellow breasted Mesánge Charbonnière,

no bigger than a sparrow, intent
on his endless chores, hurtles over
our balcony and into the aspen

repeatedly to gather insects
for the brood. His five noted song
the whirl of wings, the insistent

one note cries of hunger in that hidden nest
is the story of a few days. A week later,
I hear three notes from the chicks

and the parents have taken over the balcony,
perching on the clothesline,
their songs louder

than our conversations.
Those changes in a such short
period remind me of how rearing

my adult children when they were small,
now seems like days,
that they have flown away to far off places,

scattered in the winds,
like the children I harbored
over the years, Marie Uzumanu

from the Cameroons, Jose Arroyo,
and the Lao refugee, Vanhkam,
as difficult as a troubled teen-ager,

yet who flew off like the others
to make a new nest. Now I share
another heart-beat, the mountain's pulse.

Somalia

The child's head seems large
compared to his skeletal frame,
but his eyes are as luminous
as the sea, reflect a cloudless
sky, radiate his innocence.
In his face, distance becomes
irrelevant, and though his time
is brief, his gaze has the eternity
of sacred texts, reminding
us that there is light
and darkness in our hearts,
showing us how the world
is out of balance.

Human Landscape

Resurrection

For Phil Hasouris

There was a valley,
Le Cirque du Fer à Cheval,
surrounded by high mountains
where waterfalls gushed
from the peaks.
There was only a narrow path
by a glacial river
with its blue-green lights.
Suddenly the earth collapsed.
Hills rose at the mouth
of the entrance. Boulders
large as houses cascaded.
There were no more trees.
But years later the river
still flowed although it changed
its course and expanded,
crashing over rocks
far below jagged layers of shale.
Bulldozers moved gravel
and carved sinuous paths. The valley
opened but was altered. Hikers
returned. My friend
who lost his beloved wife
without warning, endured
the transformation of his years.
His life still flowed though
it changed its course
and he healed
the wounded on his path.

The Fluency of Shadows

I walk through the calligraphy
of tree shadows arcing on frozen lawns,
cement walks. Though the trees are stripped
bare; ash, maple, elm, oak
are writing their stories, the span of their scripts,
embodied images, dwarf
passersby. Their time's measure
is beyond us; snow, drought,
the different rhythms
of rain, but entwined with the way
we hold conflicts that enrich us,
joy, the weight of sorrow,
and like the shadows –
each curving in its own trajectory;
the running cursive, the spiritual stele,
elegiac– what we leave behind
us is palpable, wondrous,

Cancelled Flight

It is midnight and everyone is weary.
The hours too are stranded because they are all
we have in this crowded cavern where
we've waited for our luggage

after a cancelled flight.
But it's as if we were all poised on the edge
of forever with just our stories;
the man who sits down beside me

raging, *We had planned this vacation
to Crete for months and now it's all spoiled*,
the young woman with tousled hair
worrying about her small children in Zurich,

her aged mother caring for them, her father
who lives four hours away and
has Parkinson's disease, thinner and paler
every time she visits. I hold her hand,

keeping my own illness
a secret. Then a professor from Zagreb,
Zagabria, recounts the months
she spent in a cellar with her daughter

during the bombings. We curse that war
between Serbs, Croats and Muslims,
exchange photos of our children

and memories of my home city, Trieste,
she knows so well. As the conversation
ebbs, I am a teenager again in that city

when a cousin managed to visit us
from communist Yugoslavia,
regal, cigarette holder in hand,

and me wondering how she survived,
not knowing that I too would become
a traveler through life's shadows.

At the Mother Cabrini School

Ruler in hand for the wayward,
Sister Fede would have us march
in rows for chapel, for recess
and even for lunch. We were supposed to keep
silent in line yet we smirked
at each other behind her back.

She decreed there was to be
no stirring from our desks,
but our eyes kept straying towards
the clock as the words *limbo*, *purity*
and *shame* floated above our heads
and through the transom.

By noon, the classroom would be filled
with invisible butterflies, terns
and macaws, our thoughts
fluttering wildly out of the door
rehearsing our own flight
into the anarchic future.

A Silver Bracelet

Gleams inside a box, protected from the film
of years, a bracelet with a locket shaped
like a book no bigger than my thumbnail.
In it my sister's cheeks
are flaming, her eyes are laughing
(this was before her smile
was extinguished). She is telling me stories
far into the night, lilacs are foaming
in our garden and the lake at the end of our street
sighs through my window.
Someday someone will find the bracelet,
run her fingers over the flowered tracery and see
photos without a name. She will hold it
in her palm for a moment
before discarding it, not realizing
I am still inside with my lost sister,
and the lake thundering.

Bonnard's Open Door at Vernon

Swaths of orange clouds fill the open door,
A horizon's blue-green sea,
the holy nation of trees.
I see the white lilacs

of my childhood, "Russian Lilacs,"
my mother said as I first breathed in
their perfume, their miracle
canceling the city's dense

gray walls where I once leaned
on the windowsill towards
the subway's shuttered world.
But look again how a surf of miniature flowers

glistens in a field, how distances and directions
are confounded, the clouds sailing
towards us, the light etched on the windows,
glowing from inside the room.

My French Uncle

He is always the odd man out,
not because he rebels: He loves his family
of closed, prosperous burghers,
accepts their quirks like the green vein

which gives the rocquefort its flavor.
But he can't help turning
on his own axis, can never envision borders
or glass walls. In a country which loves

to calculate the weights and measures
on the social scale, he sees the world
as delight. He loves a good party,
lifting his glass as the stories bubble out,

the off-color jokes. The family is always too busy
to stop by. They never mention
the curve of his fortune;
the first wife who left him for his friend

while he was mired at the German front,
the Fraulein he brought home
after the war, when his company folded
and he moved from Paris

and bought that farm. Now at 81
he's still exploring, reading Freud and Marx.
There's always something to draw him away
from the rails. While everyone is seated

around the table, he's in the study,
adding some lines to his novel,
inventing yet another plot as he releases
himself into the spacious avenues of the beginning.

Nana's Watch

Before slipping it on its gold chain,
I wind it up with its slender wand. The spring
is still alive. I hold its ticking
against my ear like a beating heart.
May it keep singing as it journeys
from one home to another.

Invisible Light

Roses bloom in the desert,
not in oases, but in shifting veils
of sand, in the decaying urban streets
with high unemployment and rampant
prescription drug abuse, where a boy's

mother was always too dazed
by alcohol to sign him up
for free school lunches and petals
drooped in the hot wind
of his stepfather's rage until the child

moved into abandoned houses,
his life invisible as he sat
in classrooms, and the years
passed without mercy, but the roses
still bloomed when he became a man.

On the route of his delivery truck,
he met a little girl, Alliyah,
the petals blazing in her happy grin
elicited by the small gifts he left
on her doorstep because she had nothing,

and grew up learning the paths
of loneliness, then becoming
"at risk" Now Alliyah darts
through the basket- ball court
like a swallow where the man

who gifted her is a county probation
officer at a juvenile court school
where he stands tall, admonishing
yet guiding them in his protection for some

in the lottery of life, graduate

and others are sent to adult prisons.
But the gym is rinsed with invisible
light that makes roses bloom,
love radiate in the most
troubled places.

What We See

What do you say to the young girl
lying in a full length wheel chair,
covered up in blankets so all you can
see is her neck, hands that have not

developed fingers. Yet her hair
is carefully arranged in two curved
braids with bows. Her face
has its own luminosity

even though her neck can't
support her head. She is in a restaurant
with her large attentive family.
The people at other tables

avert their eyes, their conversation
lapses. They are perhaps thinking
how she can't walk out the front door,
or do much of anything. I turn around

and take her hands, telling her
that she is beautiful, for no territory
is too small for the spirit and the heart
has its own windows. I think of how

the birch tree speaks to the sky,
of how we pass by without seeing it,
unaware of the beauty that surrounds us,
the sacredness of being.

The Last Room

My mother-in-law sits in her room
barely speaking. Women tend her around the clock,
she who was once the empress
of larders and plates at *Fontenay-Sous-Bois*,

whose consort bought her jewels and an apartment
on the *Cote d'Azur* to stem her tears,
never dreaming she may have hungered
for something she couldn't name.

Her children and grandchildren appear
like April sunlight flickering in and out of clouds,
their voices as distant as her long dead husband's.
They brim with news while she stares

at what they cannot see.
So many years ago, we arrived with flowers
as newly weds but they failed
to please, kept sending her photos of our children

but they remained strangers. I tried
to conquer her wrath, bring her
over to our side not guessing there were bruises
deep inside her.

Now in my letters we discover
each other for the first time, how pain
needs no translation, how swiftly
it travels across continents and history's

switchback trails until we are like ministers
of countries that were once at war, the battles
consigned to oblivion in that great chronicle
where there are no winners or losers.

Woman With Seascape

She pauses among the rocks
where lava strides
into the Pacific with its slates and rusts,

so deep hued, the coral glows
like candles at high mass. She knows
that lingering by the ocean

on a cloudy evening is to rejoice
when a wind opens
the thick bolts, letting

a gleam of yellow script pierce
her heart, is to be ready
for astonishment, feeling her whole body

thrum. She knows that after the shouts
of reds, purples and orange
rise the quiet

drawn out strains of our passage
when the grays flow
through her, changing their lights

as velvet or watered silk does,
with gradations for every note
on the scale of feeling.

What a Pause Means

Not only on the town's busy sidewalks,
but along the paths of a college campus
shaded by maple, ash, and laurel, tall trees
bursting into green clouds after
a long winter – people are texting,
talking on cell phones, staring at Iphones,
so the world shrinks and expands
simultaneously. Have we forgotten
the music of silence, where thoughts
burgeon, memories of a mother's
voice, a family meal, a childhood
friend, the poetry of light streaming
through branches, the rain
drumming against a window, tears
that were shed? I want to tell them
to stop if only for a few minutes,
to see what is all around us,
a moment that will accompany
them as a painting, a clasped hand.

Life Prints

For Sonya Hess

This morning, I lift out a tablecloth from the depths of my linen
closet, one I haven't touched in years. A friend bought it for me
in a thrift shop because she knew that the appliquéd flowers with
their embroidered stems, the butterflies fluttering above them,
the blossoms sewed in a palette of reds, gold, and rose, would
delight me. I wonder if the artist had died, if her family, blind
to her joy in handwork, discarded her creations in second hand
stores. My friend too is long gone. Only her poetry books remain
on my shelf, silenced, although I still hear her ironic laugh,
see her writing at her makeshift desk with an ancient manual
typewriter, storing her poems in the freezer whenever she
traveled to save them in case her tiny house would burn down.
What will we leave behind us when our lives burn down like
unopened books, the things we made so lovingly discarded, our
voices but dim echoes in the ceaseless tumult of this busy world?

Journey

We drove from Makena Point at the end of the Island, haunted
with its volcanic rocks, its trees, those elders carrying ancient
stories – into a territory that is always moving, ever changing
and without boundaries, as if we were driving right into the sky
with its scudding clouds making the wind visible, some larger
than the mountains and majestically passing over the ocean,
some spreading and fanning out, as if I were seeing the universe
with its colliding stars, lights changing to burning orange, lights
that stream through the clouds, as if I too had slipped from my
homeland and time although I am made of these, and losing
swaths of memory from a brain injury has prepared me to step
out of my body and fill my eyes on the other side of pain.

Sylvia

It seems like only yesterday
that it was Christmas, your smile
in our doorway that could open windows
in the darkest rooms. You brought with you
the aroma of freshly baked cookies
as you had done for so many years.

Your gentle humor set each moment
in amber, when you once glanced at our son's
chaotic room, "You'll soon have to sleep
on the landing," or recounting your husband's
long week of hunting in New Hampshire,
"He's the only married bachelor I know!"

It seems like only yesterday, our nightly
telephone calls while you were lying
in your hospital bed, your voice
still buoyant as it charted the steady
invasion of cancer, even though
you were tethered to an oxygen tank.

On our last visit, we wore face-masks
to protect you from infection, as if it were
still possible to shield you. You were sitting up
in bed, your eyes holding a brightness
we couldn't fathom.

And then your son handing out flowers
to place on your coffin
and us drifting away, carrying
the awful weight of your absence.

Human Landscape

I walk by the bay of Sistiana at sunset
with its intimate harbor,
its somnolent pleasure boats tucked in
for the night, and families slowly
drifting back to their cars
until there's just the sea undulating
against the pilings and farther out
rows of fishing nets strung out
beneath a sky flaunting its orange shafts
through armadas of cloud.
The quay is empty now except
for two solitary figures --
a grandfather carrying his tiny grandson,
bending down so he can touch
the waves, then lifting him
onto the tip of the pilings. Together
they gaze in silence at the darkening waters
as if they had slipped out of time.

We Are Accompanied

On two Chinese wall hangings
from past centuries, the calligraphy
is sewn in shaded, multicolored silk
flowers, each with its own rhythm,
one panel dedicated to virtue that brings
longevity, the other gratitude for Divinity's
beneficence. In China centuries
were part of everyone's lives as were
ancestors and the Dao of nature, the Confucianism
of social relations, Buddha's Sutra.
They were accompanied as I am
by my forebears: my great-grandmother's
family crest my mother embossed
on a leather folder with a lamb Surrounded
by flowers and the Hapsburg flag,
a silver wine cup and vase with figures
traveling around them on horseback
from a Syrian grandmother
I never met, an angel painted on gold porcelain
that watched over my great-grandfather.
Our lives are leavened by
beauty, like the calligraphy
on the wall hangings, by listening to voices
that are not stilled, by understanding
that we are not locked in the moment
but journey like eddies in time's river.

Reverence

Hymns

I think of Falah's sister in Iraq
who lost her husband, her four children,
affectionate daughters, proud sons. I think
of her empty hands, her empty house
that is no longer a home,
and I pray.

I think there will always be wars,
cities will fracture, borders that cancel
villages, meadows and olive trees,
have their own journey,
and I pray.

I think of how one country is defined
by a sword, another by pylons
and cranes. Valleys split apart, slopes
collapse and wounds open.
Both are conquerors.
And I pray.

I think of my aunt's story, how
her mother gave her to my grandmother
as she charted her own path,
how when my aunt became a woman,
her husband married her for money
and mistreated her.

Yet she had a life, she was beautiful,
the light shone inside her.
We all have lives, the gift of time.
I pray that I may understand all that keeps
us apart, that we may learn to call each other
sister and brother, that we may learn
how the earth belongs to everyone.

The Lives of the Saints

Holy pictures of the saints
were handed out as prizes
and for reflection when I was a child
in a Catholic school.
How could I possibly submit to torture
the way they had? How could I gaze
into the distance with rapture
the way they did? I was only seven
and craved forbidden treats.

But I already learned that nothing
is what is seems – - the orthodox priest
who would pass my mother and me
as he walked our dingy streets
would reach in his pocket for candy
and place it in my mouth, knowing
it was not allowed.

Now I see saints everywhere:
they push gurneys in regulation blue
gowns, speaking Creole mixed
with English as they ferry patients.
They travel across continents,
making a human chain
to carry medicine across bombed
out bridges in Lebanon.

The holy ones patter back and forth
without letup across dreary corridors
and pavements, through the everydayness
of tragedy and need. Invisible
to the powerful, they appear
to children and to the suffering
who have learned
to see with the eyes of the heart.

Fra Angelico's Nativity

It's what we don't see --
the pulsing arc between Joseph's

raised hands and Mary's translucent fingers
fiery with love, this thrumming

of passion and wonder
like the mysterious pull

of dark matter
at the edge of our galaxy –

telling us that what shimmers
before us, the light burnishing our gestures

is only a fragment
of the vast cosmos of the heart.

Place of Worship

The only tocsins
on this mountainside
are the persistent jangling
of belled horses
and a bird plaiting
the air over hosannas
of grass.

Here there are no
greater or lesser,
no heavy robed bishops
excommunicating sheep
of different gaits
from the flock.

Here our souls
cannot be tethered
by enmity, the sky
releases its catastrophic
floods as well as
its benedictions
on everyone.

Talk Story

He tells me how the jelly fish
swarm in the ocean after a full moon,
how sharks are drawn
when the river's mouth is full,
how fishing and flowers
have their own cycle, giving me
a glimpse of all we do not see
or understand around us, how everything
is connected on this island
and its spirit. He tells me about papayas
and mangos, the fruit spilling
in his family's hands, the vitamins
that nourish us, how the trees
are part of his home at Makawao.
He tells me about a sacred place
on the promontory of the mountain;
an ancient chair surrounded
by a circle of stones where the chief
could see all the islands,
and drum out his messages
to the Big Island, summoning
a procession of canoes.
I ask him if there is a book
where I could discover more
about this island and he looks at me,
smiling at my ignorance. "There is only Talk Story."
I think how the flowers
of wisdom would bloom
in my world if we could learn
how to listen.

Hopi Ceremonial Sash

As the dance
begins,
the universe curls

around a man's
waist.
Red is the edge

followed by a surf
of clouds
raked

by equidistant
fingers
of lightening.

Then
a curtain of rain
falls,

the grass
spreading its tide.
In the friction

of air,
the dancer's flesh
shines

like a scythe.
The man feels
and does not feel

how the wind
beats on his skin
drawing him out

like sound
farther
and farther

into the paths
of swallows
and hawks.

Meeting Egypt

We met in an airport,
I never learned his name.
He had green eyes, black hair,
a pensive face. We spoke
of Naguib Mahfouz's
novels, the way life was
in Egypt. *He was just telling*
the truth, he wasn't criticizing
the government. There are those
who are quiet, those who are loud.
My grandfather taught me not to raise
my voice because it meant that I didn't know
anything. We talked about Arab poets
we both loved. He knew how art
responds to butterflies, the greens
of springtime. We both knew
that some people
see with the mind, others
with their heart, that life is short
and we each have a destiny, a role to play.
When you die, you leave behind
your family, your money. What remains
is the happiness you gave to others.

Bougainvillea

Take the bougainvillea bush,
its blazing purples, magentas, pale
orange, glittering rose, calling out
to us like a bell tower
rising on the side of a landfill
where flapping plastic bags
line the road.
Something about hope
and the colors of compassion
even in the darkest landscapes.

Addressing the Mountain

Mountain, we are two solitudes,
both distant and close.

We have done with clamorous
voices, the season's false colors.

Like the spare skin of earth
that covers your bones

I have become permeable,
I am soaked by the tears

of strangers. And what of the clouds
towering above,

giant continents sweeping past?
I tell you my love is like that:

although I am small
and of little consequence, my heart

races across years reinventing itself
with the ever shifting winds.

At the Church of St. Germain-des-Prés

I walk into the sixth century footsteps
of Clovis, the first king of France,
when Lutecia was renamed
Paris, soar beyond myself
beneath sky high arches
that draw us through their long.
trajectory. Fratricidal killings in the monarchy
are silenced. Conflicts between
Normands, Romans and Gauls
evaporate like clouds. Colors
blaze from windows in the dimness
like unfurling petals, Saints sculpted
in stone in the thirteen hundreds
beckon, Our Lady of Notre Dame bestows
her smile although centuries
have worn away sections
of her stance, and behind her
the bared stones from the initial
construction are a counterpoint to
the crowded streets that now flow
around the church. Below the aisles
were scriptoria where hour
upon hour the words, the pages
of holy books emerged to shelter us
like ancient trees and illustrations bloomed
from tireless fingers. Outside
the plaza, now emptied,
was once filled with the bustle of
the Middle Ages: passion plays
and whirling acrobats, the cries
of open air markets, the deft gestures
of thieves, students from the Sorbonne
carousing. Here joy and sorrow
life and death, are joined.

Another Vision

Nothing is what it seems, as this bewildering
and shifting world unfurls
before us. Take the family in the waiting room
at the Medical Imaging Center. There was a child
in a reclining wheelchair, but she was not
a child, although she had a small body.
She wore earrings and had an older face.
Hi Sweetheart, I called out and her father
replied, *She wants to know your name*
as if he could read her thoughts.
Nonna, I said, *it means grandmother*
in Italian. Na she sang out, *Na, Na*,
as my maternal heart lurched
with pain. But then I watched her father
leaning over her chair, his face glowing
with such tenderness, as if a thousand threads
of invisible light were holding them together,
and I remembered the ancient story about the man
who picked up a wounded creature
on the side of the road, carrying her gently
into town where everyone pointed and laughed,
not seeing the form of Buddha in his arms.
In that waiting room, with its closed faces
of boredom and worry, shone an icon of flesh
and blood, the holy child, the blessed father.

The World

Unfolds in the Paris Métro.
At Anvers, Africa enters, a tall woman
with a cloud of black hair, an orange
and green dress. As the doors slide
open a woman with a colored
headscarf, then another with a brown
one, both smiling step in. The young girl
across from me is wired, glued
to her Ipod, a young man lost
in his thoughts, a black man
wearing a tattered jacket and one
down the aisle leaning against
the window, his head drooping,
the only place he can sleep,
his homelessness unobserved.
Standing by the door is a tall man
carrying a bag, sorrow inscribed
on his features. It's late morning
after the people in suits at the station
of Saint Sulpice have rushed
to work. In fifteen minutes
I am at the crossroads of East
and West, of happiness and misery.

The Art of Living

The mind should learn to go barefoot
to see all that surrounds us,
the native Wili Wili tree
which converses with the wind,
its trunk growing horizontally
among Hawaian grasses.
Or the Melos those dancers,
trunks that flow in arcs,
branches thrusting
in all directions like elbows
holding up the sky.
They tell us how we are related
to the shifting currents
of air and water, susceptible
to wasps and fungus.
The elegant Eucalyptus
that rise vertically are strangled
by kudzu, like houses
on the mainland felled
by sub primes and securitiziation,
telling us that the heart too
should go barefoot.

Emperor Qianlong's Private Paradise

In a panel made of precious zitan wood
to reflect the fact that the plum tree
blooms for a thousand years,
a horizontal tree splays its multiple
writhing branches. Everything is in motion.
It's jade blossoms are stars
shedding tremors of light.
Even the lapis lazuli beneath the tree
bright as a summer sky
moves like the sea. On a double sided panel
flowers are dancing, their leaves
and stems speaking
their own language, their earth
a fastidiously carved sandalwood.
The emperor Qianlong is still writing
poetry, designing a garden where rocks
are mountains and branches intermingle
with roofs, a landscape
that is unpredictable and invites
discovery, where inside
and outside are confounded,.
where he retreats to a tiny room
and sits in a lotus-petalled
niche, a Buddhist sanctuary
of awareness for the lotus
with its roots in mud
rises out of murky water
revealing that a soul
regardless of its original circumstances
can reach enlightenment.

Reverence

The feather lying by my feet
while I was resting on a bench
was dark gray, immaculate.
I brought it home and placed it
on my writing table, my companion,
my messenger, telling me
that wherever we go, we leave
a gift, a murmur of assent,
as we listen to a person's story,
remember the wind's
song in the leaves, the hawks
sailing currents that bring us
to faraway places, the butterflies
rising above tall grasses
in their mating dance, the one
that accompanied me as I walked
under a canopy of trees. It waited
for me, a stillness on the gravel path,
then fluttered and landed
on the path ahead of me, over
and over. I remember the bird
that swooshed above my head,
heard its wings humming,
after my mother died in autumn
when all the birds had migrated.
Walk in silence and in solitude.
There are different ways of knowing.

Another Way of Seeing

Clouds move up the slopes until we can
no longer see what is before us.

How many of us are wrapped
in clouds, where there is only one person's

thoughts and dreams, only one person's
story. Inside each one of us

is a lamp that can illuminate
the past, an olive branch, unspoken

words. Those who wear clouds
want to name the Other,

the ones who are different,
to tell them that they do not belong –

who do not wish to see
our journey, extend their hand to those

in pain. Each one of us carries a lamp
deep inside us, that embraces

the enemy, the conqueror, the lonely
and the misunderstood.

THE TREES HOMILY

The Book of Wisdom

1

Not a pasture, but a green sea
its tall grasses, daisies, hemlocks
and fireweeds undulating
in the wind. There are no farmers,
or strangers with backpacks
and walking sticks. This is a page
in the book of life: Socrates
was made to eat hemlock
so his wisdom wouldn't annoy
the ignorant. Knowledge and friendship
are exchanged for fame. The person
who understands our thirst
for belonging, strides out
into the field and cuts down
the tallest stalk.

2

On the slope daisies and grasses
sway and curve against a wall
of sheer rock. I remember a friend
who lived through a revolution,
telling me how to endure, "Oaks
break, willows bend."

3

The rapids carve granite, schist and shale,
enter a dam with its blue sheen
where the level is maintained
by sluice gates. But glaciers
are quickly receding from the Himalayas
to the Alps, millions of acres
of wheat succumb to drought.
Our history books are filled
with wars we can ignore,
but the disregarded force of nature
is seriously wounded.

Summer

1

The seeds on their perilous journey
are bathed on the font
of the moment, the aspens
race in the wind, the burgeoning clouds
rise like a gathering of prophets.

2

But at the end of the path,
power hoes are gouging huge wounds
in the earth. The, roads, the towns
are creeping up the slopes, swallowing
meadows, dismantling the refuge
of barn swallows, the cuckoo,
the red-tailed hawk.

3

The pass at *le Col des Annes* towers
above the surge of towns
and villages. We are not contained here
where the cowbells' tocsins
sound in wave upon wave
of summer pastures, where farther up
yawn cathedrals of rock and ice,
the blueness of eternity.

Joy and Chaos

Temperatures are soaring in Trieste.
Weather is no longer predictable. At Miramare,
the gardens have no flowers because
of the unseasonable drought, yet visitors
still flock to see the castle and its terraces
leading to the Adriatic. When suddenly,
there is a heavy, relentless rain, while people
huddle on a tiny stone platform with a few
tables and chairs and a glass roof
but no walls. Suddenly a group of teenage boys,
hanging around with their instruments
take up their drum, their flute, their accordion
to begin folk music, and a dark haired man
who was keeping time beside them
with his foot tapping, invites an older woman
to dance and soon there are three couples
dancing in that tiny space, toddlers
wandering around, people who never met,
speaking to each other, and during a break,
the drummer gives his drum to a three year old
who is overjoyed and bangs away.
People clap, while many are standing
at the edge of the platform,
watching the festivities, undeterred
by the hours, the rain's message.

Children

The voices of children fill the summer air,
their cries mingling with birdsong.
They are playing in the meadow,
their loose hair indistinguishable from the yellow
field flowers, the fireweed, the paint box
of colors rising through the grass.
They are catching butterflies
and crickets; some live, some die.
They race back and forth across the grass,
the tall one always in the lead,
then pause to count their spoils,
to see who has the most, to quarrel
and regroup. They already know
so much. Yet they are children:
the afternoon will never end, the world
fits in their hands.

The Sundarbans Tiger Preserve

Here, whenever a mangrove forest dies,
the doors of the earth slam shut
taking the Smooth Indian otter,
the Irrawaddy and Gangetic dolphins,
the cheetah-spotted fishing cat
and the Royal Bengal tiger, holding
it all in his eyes' vigilance,
ruling the intricate web
like Vishnu the Preserver and Destroyer --
leaving the villages prey
to the power of cyclones.

The Plains Dreaming

The tundra where galaxies
of caribou swirl through the land, thousands
upon thousands, and currents of snow geese
spill into a bay of grasses,
a lone fox circling their nests,
sparking a flurry of squawks and wings,
the Mongolian plains where gazelles race faster
than sudden wild fires, the savannahs
where the air pulses and wisdom lies
in heightened senses, the night vision
of the lioness tracking stragglers
with her burning gaze, the grasses that die
and spring up in recurring rhythms,
the journey written in each wing beat and hoof.

Wilderness

1

When the trees sing in the stillness
the earth will unfurl its whirlwind
of feathers, the sky will release
its waters of light.

2

The monkeys in their intricate pathways
of branches, the birds in their screen
of leaves are watching us.
There are eyes all around, peering
through the brush,
taking our measure.

3

The thunder is coming out
of the morning mist, making the plains
vibrate as wildebeests tumble on
in a river of muscle and sinew.
Listen, there are no walls
between us, only
this drumming in the blood.

Poem for Guy Muffat

You're only a farmer chasing his sheep up the slopes.
Why remember you when there are hikers
in suede boots and purple jackets,
siren peaks touted by the travel magazines?

Because I prefer the plowed fields
of your face, your worn sweater,
your blue-green eyes burning
with an anguish no one sees.
Because of the difficult winters

late springs when there was barely enough grass
for the sheep, yet somehow you held on.
Because you raged when they entered your fields
without warning and tore out all the pines
to make room for ski-lifts.

Because you grieve for the trees: perhaps it's easier
than grieving for the sons who gave up
and moved into town. Because
when they rip up the mountain
to make up a new road

they're tearing your flesh. Because you stand alone
before the mayor, the municipal council,
and the rising tide of vacation homes,
trying to hold the line
in your own hands.

Combloux

When I saw the tall grass, the field flowers raise
their yellow heads beside the parking for ski buses,
when I saw the aspen fluttering in the wind like
a flock of birds and horses browsing, I was misled.
The Mt. Blanc with its silvery mantle, its blue-green
glaciers that once soared above the villages like a
benevolent planet reminding us that we are just a spark
in the great river of light, is sloughing off its royal
robes. Gray peaks jut out, shoulders of rock with
a few ragged white patches, as if the Mt. Blanc
had moved closer with its scars. Nothing escapes us now.

Pay Attention

to what's   around you,
heavy clouds   scudding past
making   the wind
visible   each with its own
shape   its own speed,
wind   that comes
more often   now
confusing   the migration
of wings

branches   running
in place   on a birch
that is   dying
because a stream
has been   diverted

a bee   that is losing
its power   of flight
and tumbles in a hedge

there is   no safety
behind   a wall
open the windows

of your eyes   heart   mind
listen   to the trees
singing the earth's homily

Two Profiles

Larch, aspen, blue spruce, hold
the sky in their branches, Each one
draws life from its roots,

their language circulating
beneath the ground,
is a community of murmurs; trilling

birds, wind- riffling leaves,
is a book of memories
whose terrain holds weathered farmers

shepherds, intimates of the mountain.
Descending the narrow path
is entering a cathedral,

its green leafed arches,
the joyous hymns of crickets,
the holy water of cascading

streams over rocks. While on the lower
slopes, cranes, architects of desire,
are multiplying over mounds

of dirt. Crowded together, chalets
are a new forest covering the slopes,
for the ski season.

May we remember the Popul Vuh,
the Mayans' creation story, that the sky
has a heart as does the earth.

Monet's Homage

1

In reflections of a willow
with its lavender glow,
a man's profile, his hands
barely visible are part
of the lower trunk
and behind the tree,
is a pale outline of a house.
As we age, our visions
of the world deepen.
We understand that we are
part of and respect
what surrounds us.

2

The pulsating earth we despoil,
emanates light; oranges, crimsons,
yellows everywhere, its secrets
woven into all that surrounds us.
A tree vibrates, its presence
defined by strong brush strokes,
Monet understood
as did Australian aborigines
that "trees think."

3

Fire and water flow
into each other, beneath the stillness
of lily pads. The cathedral, pure
gold, soars above the purple strip
that is Rouen as if we were hearing
the choir sing that we must
walk in light and wisdom.

4

Across the Seine, the Paris skyline
is illuminated in the palest mauves
and pinks, with variations
of white in the foreground,
a mystical moment that will
never fade.

5

There are no beginnings, no endings,
no boundaries in the abundance
of meadows, wisterias rising
below a bridge in blazing stalagmites.
Rock formations throb
in writhing seas. The earth
is sacred. It's powerful visions
call out to us in a dark world.

About the Author

Marguerite Guzmán Bouvard was for many years a professor of Political Science and director of poetry workshops at Regis College, and has been a writer in residence at the University of Maryland. She is multidisciplinary and has published 19 books including 8 books of poetry, and numerous books and articles in the fields of Political Science, Psychology, Spirituality and Literature. Her first poetry book won the Quarterly Review of Literature Award, her seventh, the MassBook Award for Poetry. She has served as editor of Healing Ministry Magazine. Both her poetry and essays have been widely anthologized. She has received fellowships at the Radcliffe Institute and the Wellesley College Center for Research on Women and grants for her poetry from the Puffin and Danforth foundations. She is a Resident Scholar at the Women's Studies Research Center, Brandeis University.

Made in the USA
Charleston, SC
07 August 2015